THEATRE YEAR

A selection of photographs by Donald Cooper of productions in London and Stratford October 1982 to September 1983.

With an introduction and index by Michael Coveney.

In (Parenthesis) Limited

To E.T., for Earthly Guidance

Front cover:
Roger Rees *Henry*; Felicity Kendal *Annie*
The Real Thing Strand Theatre

The dates listed refer to the official Press nights. Every
effort has been made to ensure the accuracy of the
information given.

Published by In (Parenthesis) Limited
21 Wellington Street, London WC2

Printed in England by Battley Brothers Printers, Clapham, London SW4 0JN
Designed by Michael Morris

Introduction
**By Michael Coveney,
theatre critic of the Financial Times.**

The pound sterling tumbled against the American dollar with the result that, by the middle of an unusually warm and agreeable London summer, the tourists flocked back and the business picked up. There were even reports of half a dozen shows in the West End being entirely sold out. *Cats* purred along on both sides of the Atlantic, re-couping its entire Broadway investment by early August. At the end of the same month in London, there was no ticket available for the show until January 1984.

The composer of *Cats*, Andrew Lloyd Webber, turned producer for one of the year's hits, the exuberant schoolgirl pastiche *Daisy Pulls It Off*, and suddenly announced, after being thwarted last year in his bids to acquire first the Aldwych and then the Old Vic, that he had purchased the freehold on the Palace Theatre, a magnificent monument of high Victorian art on Cambridge Circus. The Palace's boss for the past 37 years, Sir Emile Littler, now 80, wisely but sadly declared that it was no good owning a theatre unless you had something worthwhile to present in it.

Residents and visitors alike continued to vote with their credit cards for the National Theatre – which had a poor year in comparison with 1982 – and the Royal Shakespeare's new London home in the Barbican. Audiences obviously do not mind high ticket prices so long as they can park, drink, eat and go to the loo in comparative comfort. Only the first of these tasks remains daunting at the Barbican. West End facilities, on the whole, are still disgraceful. I ascended to the street after Glenda Jackson's show at the Vaudeville through an exit staircase which smelt like a urinal.

Last year's RSC Stratford-upon-Avon season arrived at the Barbican trailing clouds of well-earned glory, although the best revival of *King Lear* since Peter Brook's of twenty years ago was scandalously under-exploited because Michael Gambon could not resist crossing the Thames to take the lead in the new Christopher Hampton play at the National. The turn-over in both our major subsidised companies remains prodigious, not to say reckless, and scheduling arrangements seem incapable of finding ways to prolong the active life of the best shows.

I hope we have not seen the last of the RSC's marvellous *Peter Pan*, a real Christmas treat served up by the *Nicholas Nickleby* production team and containing, in Jane Carr's Wendy, one of the year's most remarkable performances. The directors, John Caird and Trevor Nunn, plundered the 1928 text, Barrie's 1911 novel, even the 1920 film scenario. They rejected the travesty tradition in the title role and made you wonder why on earth it had survived for so long. Miles Anderson's Peter was drawn to Wendy as a maternal surrogate and the crunch came when Miss Carr, maturing visibly to womanhood, realised that this was *all* that was required of her.

In a year when Giles Cooper's *Happy Family* was revived and Peter Tinniswood's *You Should See Us Now* delightfully demonstrated, with an adult cast, that the child was father to the child, a *Peter Pan* stripped of pantomimic encrustation was revealed as both gripping yarn and masterful study of the infant psyche.

Stephen Moore as a J M Barrie narrator figure drew our atten-tion to the frightening ability of children to inflict pain while behaving naturally. Mercifully, this device did not interfere with the sensual delights of the production: breathtaking effects, designed by John Napier, included the best high flying system yet devised for the legitimate stage; a blue lagoon of billowing shot silk through which little heads bobbed and peeped like ripples in the sunlight; and a Neverland which was a grassy knoll of gnarled treestumps, exotic blooms, fantastic animals and inviting hidey-holes.

Another highspot in the Barbican year was a rumbustious revival of *The Roaring Girl*. Full weight was given to some remarkable sub-plots, with outstanding work from Helen Mirren and Jonathan Hyde. Mirren played the pipe-smoking cutpurse Moll as a street hero on the run from the implications of her own sexuality, and Barry Kyle's production, although a little over imitative perhaps of what now seem like RSC *Nickleby* conventions, presented a teeming picture of Jacobean London bristling with sexual innuendo, naughty deed and raucous pun. Playing in tandem with Kyle's *The Taming of the Shrew* from Stratford, this was the classical theatre in fascinatingly feminist mood. A fine season was triumphantly topped with Terry Hands' revival of *Cyrano de Bergerac*, Derek Jacobi resonantly confirming his new-won RSC star status.

A string of excellent shows in the RSC's The Other Place rescued the summer Stratford season from the ordinary, although, in the main house, *Twelfth Night* and *Henry VIII* were well up to scratch. Both of these revivals had soundtracks by the ubiquitous Ilona Sekacz, the first melancholically rainswept, the second ostentatiously Weillian.

A great wizened tree dominated John Caird's view of Illyria, imposing, without too much strain, a visual neo-Classical order on the proceedings; while Howard Davies eschewed the traditional spectacular approach to Shakespeare's last play, unravelled as best he could the complex plotting to good effect and, in Richard Griffiths' impetuously broody monarch, offered a sharp contrast to the bluff King Hal blueprint of Holbein via Charles Laughton.

Much was made in some quarters of Peter Hall's decision to present at the National in November a musical by Marvin (*A Chorus Line*) Hamlisch about the tragic film star Jean Seberg. The powerful Broadway producers, the Shuberts, have a stake in the show, as they did in *Amadeus*. Should a theatre sponsored by the taxpayer be so blatantly involved in commercial enterprise? The answer seems to me that, as long as everything is open to question by board and public alike, and that the National balances its books, it does not much matter. I would prefer plaintiffs at the court of Sir Peter (whose memoirs, due for publication late in the year, promised to be required, even painful reading for his critics) to couch their objections in terms other than merely envious or moralistic.

Nor did I join the chorus of killjoys who denounced Hall's sabbatical in Bayreuth. I do feel, though, that had he not been abroad, Michael Bogdanov would not have been allowed to get away with his awful ten-minute epilogue to an uneven production of *You Can't Take It With You*. This implicated a distinctly ragbag cast in a 1930s song and dance medley executed with the efficiency and pezazz of an early run-through by the Town's Women's Guild Amateur Dramatic and Operatic Society. Who needed it anyway?

Bogdanov's other big NT show was *Lorenzaccio* which, in my view, was as pitifully wide of the mark of de Musset as was *You Can't Take It With You* insulting to Kaufman and Hart. Some of the fault lay with second-rate casting, but most of it was down to the sheer incompetence of the staging. For once, designer John Gunter failed to save the day, leaving actors to trail off in mid-sentence as they scurried for the safety of grey surrounding drapes in the shadow of two huge marbly statues. The sinister darkness of Musset's romanticist imagination was entirely lacking and I detected little intellectual impetus behind the presentation of one of the great revolutionary dramas.

A similar vagueness of purpose invaded other areas of the NT repertoire. What on earth, for instance, was Harold Pinter up to in his tepid revival of Giraudoux's *The Trojan War Will Not Take Place*? Martin Jarvis was grossly mis-cast as Hector and most of the actors stood around looking faintly ridiculous in Greek sandals and a job lot of cocktail dresses and pleated mini-skirts. The actresses looked uncomfortable, too. Could this possibly be the play once described by Tynan as "the highest peak in the mountain-range of modern French theatre"? Other dud National revivals included Marston's *The Fawn* and de Filippo's *Inner Voices* which not even Ralph Richardson could rescue from tedium. The director of *Inner Voices*, Mike Ockrent, had enjoyed a much more robust success with another Filippo, *Ducking Out*, at Greenwich.

At least the National had two of the year's three best plays: David Hare's *A Map of the World* and Christopher Hampton's *Tales from Hollywood*. Neither was a world première, each having been seen in the same month, March 1982, in Australia and Los Angeles respectively. The Hare piece was set in a Bombay luxury hotel where a UNESCO conference on world poverty is taking place. A left wing English journalist locks competitive horns with a sleek right wing Indian novelist in a debate for the prize of an American actress's body. In a series of wonderful shifts in stage time and reality, it becomes clear we are witnessing a film being made of the confrontation as recalled by the novelist six year afterwards. Roshan Seth was superb as the novelist, Diana Quick perhaps a shade too convincingly intelligent as the actress. The problem, not really solved, was making her sacrificial offer sound not too ludicrous.

The play fizzed and sparkled, and although one or two critics refused point blank to be enmeshed in the complex theatrical structure, no-one who saw it, or rather no-one I talked to who saw it, failed to be engaged or stimulated by its arguments, its discussion of liberal attitudes towards the Third World, its bold physical metaphors of the distortion of truth in art. The final irony was that the novelist has arrived on the film set to complain about the fictional transposition to another medium of his own fiction.

A similar mulling over of artistic impulse was ingeniously dramatised in Hampton's look at the German emigrés to Hollywood before and during the last War. Michael Gambon was our shambling but precisely modulated guide in the role of Ödön von Horváth, who was not in fact one of the emigrés, being dead at the time and therefore fully licensed to roam quizzically among the twilight zones of rivalry and debate. Hampton made Horváth a hack screenwriter, slyly echoing his own recent frustrations in the cinema industry. The artist in exile is a perennially appropriate subject, never more so than today.

Hampton's script, like Hare's, is a joy to read. But, also like Hare's, it achieved in performance a confident theatrical dimension. Horváth is drawn towards the older Mann, Heinrich, while Thomas basks in his reputation on a higher plane; and the predatory, gleefully vulpine Brecht of Ian McDiarmid provided the self-deprecatory Horváth with an excuse to challenge, in the nimblest possible way, his theatrical theories.

A Map of the World and *Tales from Hollywood* prospered because of the scale of conception, the wit of the writing, the importance of the subject matter. Tom Stoppard came a good third behind his younger colleagues with *The Real Thing* at the Strand. The themes and the tone could be conveniently summarised in a slogan from the play, "Save the gerund and screw the whale." Roger Rees and Felicity Kendal were brilliantly matched as a laconic playwright and his wife who rocks the marital boat by championing a convicted hooligan's terrible play. Overlapping with Hare and Hampton, Stoppard entertainingly posed the contemporary conundrum of talent versus commitment. Henry is attacked by his wife: "Even when you write *about* something, you have to think up something to write about just so you can keep on writing. More well chosen words nicely put together. So what?"

Had the hooligan emerged as a ferociously articulate apologist for content over style, instead of as an easily derided yobbo (as was the case), the play would have been that much richer. Still, Peter Wood's production was exquisitely paced and inflected. Henry's credo, and presumably Stoppard's, was contained in the already famous cricket bat speech, in which the writer eloquently suggests that ideas in the theatre are best served if bounced off a hard, sprung surface, expertly manipulated by their proponent.

Peter Wood then moved across to the National to direct the best production there all year, *The Rivals*. Geraldine McEwan's Mrs Malaprop was as enterprising a reclamation of the role as was Judi Dench's last year of Lady Bracknell. And John Gunter redeemed himself with a recreation of the Royal Crescent in Bath which magnificently incorporated scaled-down terraces, stuccoed interiors and the cluttered cubby holes of Jack Absolute and Bob Acres.

Two new plays at the Royal Court which remained talked about all year in spite of indifferent reviews were Howard Barker's *Victory* and Robert Holman's *Other Worlds*. The plaudits flew about for Max Stafford-Clark's production of *Falkland Sound/Voces de Malvinas* in the Theatre Upstairs and for *Woza Albert!* which, like its superior prototype *Sizwe Banzi is Dead* ten years ago, fetched up in the West End after doing the rounds. Both shows expressed admirable liberal sentiments with which their audiences heartily concurred. As pieces of theatre, both bored me rigid.

Other new plays that remain fresh in the memory are Michael Wilcox's *Lent*, Caryl Churchill's *Fen*, Beth Henley's *Crimes of the Heart* and, especially, A R Gurney's *The Dining Room* at Greenwich. This latter was, in Alan Strachan's finely-honed production on a classically austere set of a Georgian room by Bernard Culshaw, a wonderfully glancing evocation of the WASP way of life in a space that had seen generations come and go. The evening had class, cool and penetrative social observation. It was performed by a well-orchestrated ensemble of reliable players, many of them associated with the work of Ayckbourn.

Arnold Wesker wrote a haunting trilogy of monologues for one of our leading young players, Nichola McAuliffe – *Annie Wobbler* played briefly at the New End in Hampstead after its première at the Birmingham Rep. There was a most productive collaboration between the writer Doug Lucie and the director Mike Bradwell on *Hard Feelings*, about lifestyles in the early '80s in the shadow of the Brixton riots. And Snoo Wilson gave some oomph to the fraying fringe with *Loving Reno* at the Bush Theatre, a highly intelligent and entertaining piece about incest and magic.

The fringe, however, as a visit to the Edinburgh Festival confirmed, is now mostly to do with radical alternative comedians scooping up contracts with trendy television producers. Of the cabaret groups, the Flying Pickets lead the field, hotly pursued by the Bouncing Czechs and Pookiesnackenburger. The minimalist, escapist phenomenon is best represented this year by the National Theatre of Brent's *The Messiah* in which two actors and a Handel-turning opera singer conjure, in delightfully irreverent vein, the Biblical prelude to the Nativity. This is a sophisticated advance on the techniques pioneered by Mike Alfreds' Shared Experience troupe, a company which now, in a strange way, shows signs of expanding in ambition beyond its capacity to do so.

One fringe play that translated successfully to the West End (although nobody except the critics really wanted to see it) was *Crystal Clear*, about emotional *angst* among the blind. The opening scene in which a partially sighted diabetic brought home to his scruffy apartment a girfriend – on, as it were, a blind date – was almost unwatchably moving. Five short, powerful scenes, originated in improvisational conditions, engaged us fully in the plight of people pushed inexorably to the edge of various predicaments. Small in scale but highly charged, the show proved beyond the salvation of critical drums loudly beaten.

It was not an outstanding year for musicals in the West End, Willy Russell's highly enjoyable *Blood Brothers* being the honourable exception. This was a sort of Liverpudlian amalgam of *Il trovatore, Twelfth Night* and Trevor Griffiths' *Sam Sam*. Barbara Dickson, with all the vocal and charismatic quality of a young Gracie Fields, was the mother of twins separated at birth and subjected to contrasting social circumstances. A contagiously melodious score by Mr Russell (expertly arranged by Pete Filleul) invoked, at key points, the legend of Marilyn Monroe, which is more than could be said of the musical that set out to celebrate her directly. *Marilyn!* (only the producers could possibly, and with difficulty, defend the exclamation mark) was a lamentable piece of broken-backed hagiography.

Topol returned in his most famous role of Tevye the milkman in *Fiddler on the Roof* at the Apollo Victoria (28 6 83), fully justifying his pension from the part, and Tommy Steele went down with all gums blazing in a crude, technically tasteless but full-value sock-it-to-'em stage version (why bother?) of *Singin' in the Rain* at the Palladium (30 6 83).

Hand on heart, the musical I most enjoyed all year was Sondheim's *Merrily We Roll Along* as performed by a group of music and drama students at the Bloomsbury. Not only the story, but also the score, makes wickedly clever use of the flashback device, and gained enormously from being performed by ebullient youngsters on the threshold of both lives and careers. The musical, prompted by the return of a disillusioned, distinguished middle-aged composer to his alma mater, is a cynical catalogue of the dangers that lie ahead, given brilliantly optimistic counterpoint by the freshness of the cast itself. Is *Merrily* doomed to the same fate as *Follies* and *Pacific Overtures* (now *there's* one for the National) and to be denied a professional showing in London?

The most surprising, and for that matter most outstanding, production in the commercial sector was Keith Hack's of Botho Strauss's *Great and Small*. The media, following reports of disaster in the provinces, were anxious to saddle Glenda Jackson with a flop to match Peter O'Toole's in *Macbeth* even before it opened. In fact, the play was a fast and very funny series of vignettes compiled around the fate of one who, in the parlance of the day, is termed a bag lady. A mutterer among the plastic detritus of everyday middleclass urban life, Jackson gave what I shall recall in future years as one of her very best performances, ably abetted by

a superb cast (Barry Stanton notable among them) and a wonderfully confident production. It was fresh, it was different, it was ambitious.

And it was presented by the producer of the year, Duncan Weldon, whose Triumph Apollo organisation also brought to the Haymarket Rex Harrison and Diana Rigg in *Heartbreak House;* Peter O'Toole and Lisa Harrow in *Man and Superman;* Beryl Reid and Donald Sinden in *The School For Scandal*; and Alan Bates in the sumptuous Chichester revival of Osborne's *A Patriot For Me*. Bates gave a fascinating display of political and sexual ambiguity as a corrupted officer of the Austro-Hungarian empire. A great play was restored, and not before time, to the English stage. For one thing it reminded us – some are quick to forget – that Osborne is a brilliantly gifted playwright; for another, it nailed the canard that, as a playwright, he knows nothing about structure.

Triumph Apollo also presented Peter Ustinov's somewhat bumbling *Beethoven's Tenth* (Ustinov remains one of the few stars guaranteed to sell out anything he appears in, even a play of his own) and the quite dreadful *Cowardice* starring Ian McKellen and Janet Suzman. It may be deduced from this slight indication of the management's activities that Triumph Apollo are certainly the most pervasive new tenants in the West end, if not exactly the new Tennent's. Inconsistency of style and wavering artistic judgement so far forbid comparison with the greatest of commercial managements.

Other performances worth celebrating are those of Warren Mitchell in *Ducking Out*, Dario Fo in his sensational one-man show which came to the Riverside Studios, Ben Kingsley as Kean, Cheryl Campbell in *Miss Julie*, Denis Lawson in *Mr Cinders* (a revival whose charm disintegrated on leaving the pocket handkerchief stage of the King's Head), Griff Rhys Jones in *Charley's Aunt*, and last, but by absolutely no means least, Frances de la Tour and Ian Bannen in the Riverside's strong production of O'Neill's *A Moon For the Misbegotten* (21 6 83).

The last hour or so of *Moon* saw de la Tour and Bannen tread warily around the banality of the text to create a truly memorable symphony for two voices: she, patiently long-suffering but galvanised as he, drunk and pathetic in the moonlight, unleashed the buried guilt of having slept with a whore on the same train that carried his mother's corpse home for burial.

Moon transferred to the Mermaid (9 9 83) after the long and successful run of *Trafford Tanzi* (which, if you really want to know, I hated) came to an end. In between, the Mermaid trustees finally gave the boot to the man who built the theatre, but ran up a few debts, Bernard Miles. Miles was sadly resigned to the fact that, in the grim concrete development which now houses his buried dream child, there is more money to be made in bingo halls or squash courts than in theatres.

Lord Miles departed stoically to resume, at the age of 76, a long-neglected acting career, bound for the West End in Lindsay Anderson's production of *The Cherry Orchard* alongside Joan Plowright and Frank Finlay. The cruel irony was that he played Firs, the senile retainer who is left alone on the estate as the family moves out and the modern drama's first property speculator moves in to mutilate the orchard and maximise the land's profitable potential.

1 *A Kind of Alaska:* Judi Dench *Deborah*; Paul Rogers *Hornby*

2 Paul Copley *Bob*; Lesley Manville *Sue*; Joanne Whalley *Rita*

Rita, Sue and Bob Too Royal Court 20 10 82

3 Penelope Wilton *Barbara Undershaft*; Siân Phillips *Lady Britomart*

Major Barbara Lyttelton 27 10 82

4 Brewster Mason *Andrew Undershaft*; Nicholas Jones *Adolphus Cusins*

Major Barbara Lyttelton 27 10 82

5 Alan Tilvern *Judge Murdoch*; Anne Twomey *Claudia*

Nuts Whitehall 2 11 82

6 Warren Mitchell *Len Coppell*

Ducking Out Greenwich 9 11 82

7 Barbara Kinghorn *Emily Creed*; Isabel Dean *Ellen Creed*;
Gillian Raine *Louisa Creed*

Ladies in Retirement Fortune Thriller Theatre 9 11 82

8

A Handful of Dust Lyric Theatre Hammersmith 10 11 82

9 Christopher Whitehouse *Maxwell*; John Keegan *Pat O'Connor*; Walter McMonagle *McClay*

Diary of a Hunger Strike Round House 11 11 82

10 Felicity Kendal *Annie*; Roger Rees *Henry*

The Real Thing Strand 16 11 82

11

The Dead Class Riverside 17 11 82

12 Peter O'Toole *John Tanner*; James Grout *Roebuck Ramsden*; Lisa Harrow *Ann Whitefield*

Man and Superman Theatre Royal, Haymarket 18 11 82

13 part 1: *The Slab Boys*: Gerard Kelly *Spanky Farrell*; Iain Andrew *Hector McKenzie*; Billy McColl *Phil McCann*; Nicholas Sherry *Alan Downie*

Paisley Patterns/The Slab Boys Trilogy Royal Court 18 11 82

14 part 2: *Cuttin' A Rug*: Iain Andrew *Hector*; Billy McColl *Phil*; Stella Gonet *Bernadette*; Gerard Kelly *Spanky*; Jennifer Piercey *Miss Walkinshaw*

15 part 3: *Still Life*: Elaine Collins *Lucille*

Paisley Patterns/The Slab Boys Trilogy Royal Court 22 11 82 24 11 82

16 Fiona Fullerton *Guenevere*; Richard Harris *King Arthur*

Camelot Apollo Victoria 23 11 82

17 Susan Fleetwood *Titania*; Paul Scofield *Oberon*

A Midsummer Night's Dream Cottesloe 25 11 82

18 Sheila Steafel

Steafel Variations Apollo 7 12 82

19 Pauline Siddle; Patricia Marks *Tanta Rose*; Matyelok Gibbs *Rebecca*; Maureen Lipman *Rachel*

20 Jim Broadbent *Pat*; Gemma Jones *Win*; Fred Pearson *Bert*; Janet Dale *Micky*

Clay The Pit 14 12 82

21 Simon Gipps-Kent *Sebastian*; Emily Richard *Viola*

Twelfth Night Donmar Warehouse 15 12 82

22 Jane Booker *Diana Lake*; Clive Francis *Lt-Commander Rogers*

French Without Tears Greenwich 16 12 82

23 Jane Carr *Wendy*; Miles Anderson *Peter Pan*

Peter Pan Barbican 16 12 82

24 Sarah Brightman *Nightingale*

Nightingale Lyric Hammersmith 22 12 82

25 Glyn Grain *Garry Lejeune*; Gabrielle Drake *Belinda Blair*; Robert Bathurst *Tim Allgood*; Phyllida Law *Dotty Otley*; John Quayle *Frederick Fellowes*

26 Robert Flemyng *Selsdon Mowbray*; Mandy Perryment *Brooke Ashton*;
Benjamin Whitrow *Lloyd Dallas*

27 Graham Hoadly *Lumley*; Denis Lawson *Jim*; Philip Bird *Guy*

Mr Cinders Kings Head 5183

28 Beryl Reid *Mrs Candour*

29 Donald Sinden *Sir Peter Teazle*

The School for Scandal Theatre Royal, Haymarket 61 83

30 The McGann Brothers

Yakety Yak! Astoria 10 1 83

31 Cheryl Campbell *Miss Julie*

Miss Julie Lyric Hammersmith Studio 17 1 83

32 Julian Hough; Patrick Barlow

The Messiah Tricycle 19 1 83

33 Susan Colverd *Ma Ubu*; Chris Barnes *Pa Ubu*

The Vandalist Donmar Warehouse 25 1 83

34 David Anderson *Clerk of Court*; Terry Neason *Mary McKinley*

Any Minute Now . . . Theatre Royal, Stratford East 26 1 83

35 Chris Barnes *Sancho Panza*; Russell Enoch *Don Quixote*

Quixote Donmar Warehouse 26 1 83

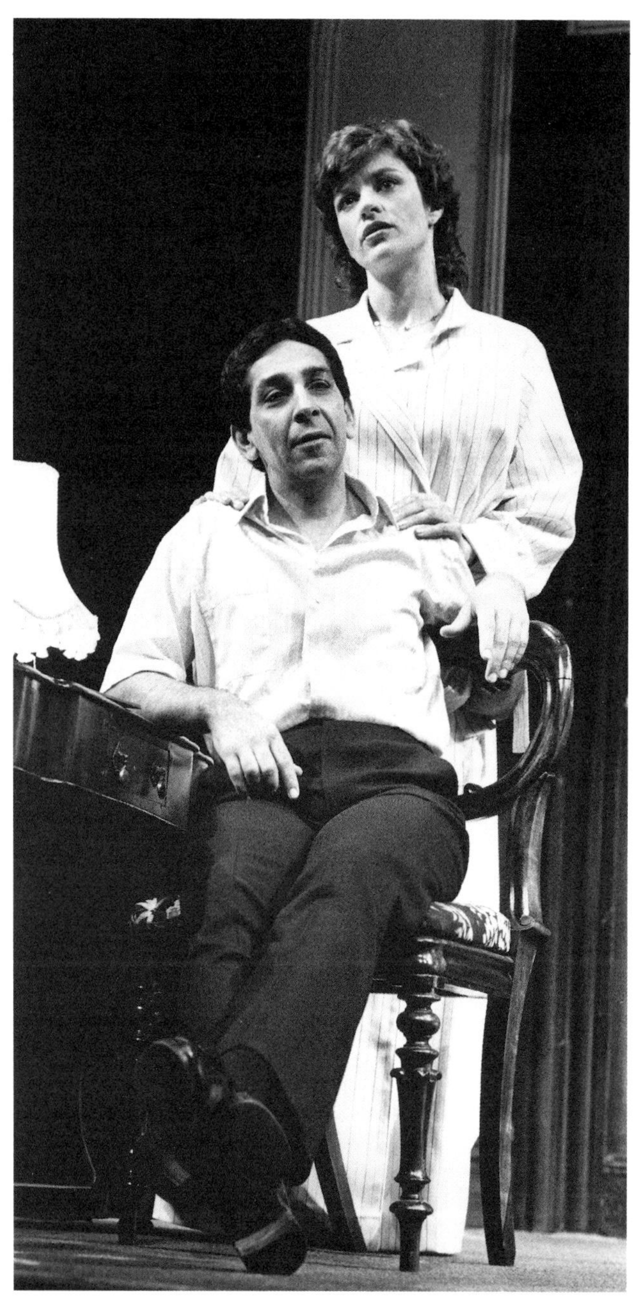

36 Roshan Seth *Victor Mehta*; Diana Quick *Peggy Whitton*

A Map of the World Lyttelton 27 1 83

37 Simon Cadell *Ernest*; Christopher Cazenove *Graham*; Delia Lindsay *Pamela*

You Should See Us Now Greenwich 31 1 83

38 Diana Katis *Annie*; Ian Reddington *Rusty*; Frances Barber *Viv*

Hard Feelings Bush 3 2 83

39 Anita Dobson *Kitty Verdun*; Griff Rhys Jones *Lord Fancourt Babberley*; Briony McRoberts *Amy Spettigue*

Charley's Aunt Lyric Hammersmith 9 2 83

40 Helen Cooper; Lucy Burge

41 Laurie Anderson: in rehearsal

United States I-IV Dominion 16 2 83

42 James Hazeldine *Jim*; Kenneth Cranham *Joe*; Jane Lapotaire *Eileen*

Kick for Touch Cottesloe 15 2 83

43 James Hazeldine *Gerard*; June Watson *Mrs Harte*; Maggie Steed *Mrs Driscoll*; Phillip Joseph *Vincent*

Small Change Cottesloe 23 2 83

44 Jonathan Kent *Paul Blake*; Wensley Pithey *Mr Maitland*

Lent Lyric Hammersmith Studio 28 2 83

45 Anthony Allen *Richard*; Diana Barrett *Jane*

46 Diana Rigg *Hesione Hushabye*; Rex Harrison *Captain Shotover*

Heartbreak House Theatre Royal, Haymarket 10 3 83

47 Noele Gordon *Mrs Sally Adams*

Call Me Madam Victoria Palace 14 3 83

48 Greg Hicks *Lorenzo (Lorenzaccio) de Medici*; Clive Arrindell *Alexander de Medici*

Lorenzaccio Olivier 15 3 83

49 Robin Summers *Matti Altonen*; Barry Stanton *Jan Puntila*

Mr Puntila and his servant Matti Tricycle 16 3 83

50 Stephanie Lawrence *Norma Jean/Marilyn*

Marilyn! Adelphi 17 3 83

51 Ian McKellen *Terry*; Glyn Owen *David*

Short List Hampstead Theatre 21 3 83

52 centre: Nigel Terry *Charles Stuart*

Victory Royal Court 25 3 83

53 Joseph O'Conor *Julius Caesar*; John Dicks *Casca*

Julius Caesar Royal Shakespeare Theatre, Stratford 29 3 83

54 Daniel Massey *Joe*; Zoë Wanamaker *Kitty Duval*

55 Barbara Dickson *Mrs Johnstone*

Blood Brothers Lyric 11 4 83

56 Patrick Ryecart *Captain Jack Absolute*; Michael Hordern *Sir Anthony Absolute, Bart.*

57 Ben Kingsley *Edmund Kean*

Edmund Kean Lyric Hammersmith 15 4 83

58 centre: Alexandra Mathie *Daisy Meredith*; Helena Little *Trixie Martin*

59 Emrys James *Malvolio*; Daniel Massey *Sir Andrew Aguecheek*; John Thaw
Sir Toby Belch; Stanley Page *Fabian*

Twelfth Night Royal Shakespeare Theatre, Stratford 20 4 83

60 Ken Jones *Jim*; Patricia Routledge *Hilda*

When the Wind Blows Whitehall 21 4 83

61 Anthony Higgins *Second Mining Engineer*; Ian McNeice *First Mining Engineer*

The White Glove Lyric Hammersmith Studio 25 4 83

62 David Troughton *Sebastian Wengrave*; Helen Mirren *Moll*; Katy Behean *Mary Fitz-Allard*

63

The Roaring Girl Barbican 26 4 83

64 Jonathan Hyde *Laxton*   65 Helen Mirren *Moll*

The Roaring Girl Barbican 26 4 83

67 Christopher Benjamin *Archie Gross*; Tom Mannion *the body*

The Body The Pit 29 4 83

68 Nicola Pagett *Helen*; Martin Jarvis *Hector*

The Trojan War Will Not Take Place Lyttelton 10 5 83

69 Lesley Dunlop *Mary*

Other Worlds Royal Court 11 5 83

70 Clare James *Mary Flynn*; Bernard Wright *Charles Kringas*; Deborah Poplet *Beth Spencer*; Hutton Cobb *Franklin Shepard*

Merrily We Roll Along Bloomsbury 11 5 83

71 Wendy Morgan *Babe Botrelle*; Amanda Redman *Meg MaGrath*; Brenda Blethyn *Lenny MaGrath*

Crimes of the Heart Bush 18 5 83

72 Peter Ustinov *Ludwig*

Beethoven's Tenth Vaudeville 19 5 83

73

Bugsy Malone Her Majesty's 26 5 83

74 Marcia Warren; Michael J. Shannon

The Dining Room Greenwich 2 6 83

75 left: Elizabeth MacLennan *Maggie Morrison*

Men Should Weep Theatre Royal, Stratford East 2 6 83

76 Julian Wadham *David*; Paul Jesson *Hugh*

77 Gemma Jones *Katherine of Aragon*

Henry VIII Royal Shakespeare Theatre, Stratford 14 6 83

78 John Thaw *Cardinal Wolsey*

79 Richard Griffiths *Henry VIII*

Henry VIII Royal Shakespeare Theatre, Stratford 14 6 83

80 Mbongeni Ngema; Percy Mtwa

Woza Albert! Criterion 15 6 83

81 Ralph Richardson *Alberto Saporito*

Inner Voices Lyttelton 16 6 83

82 James Aubrey *King Berenger the First*; Gayle Hunnicutt *Queen Marie*

Exit the King Lyric Hammersmith Studio 20 6 83

83 Jane Booker *Lady Alworth*; Emrys James *Sir Giles Overreach*;
Lewis Jones *Lord Lovell*; Anthony O'Donnell *Marrall*

84 Miles Anderson *Welborne*

A New Way to Pay Old Debts The Other Place 22 6 83

85 Dixie Carter *Liz Conlon*; Vincent Gardenia *Wild Bob Culhane*

Buried Inside Extra Royal Court 23 6 83

86 Arturo Brachetti

Y Piccadilly 27 6 83

Mizu No Eki ICA 29 6 83

88 Diane Fletcher *Catherine Winslow*; Barbara Jefford *Grace Winslow*; Jason Lake *Ronnie Winslow*; Ian Hogg *Sir Robert Morton*; Alan MacNaughtan
Arthur Winslow

The Winslow Boy Lyric Hammersmith 1 7 83

89 Connie Booth *Agatha Posket*; John Mills *Mr Posket*

Little Lies Wyndham's 12 7 83

90 James Hayes *Don Zuccone*; Bernard Lloyd *Hercules*

The Fawn Cottesloe 14 7 83

91 Sarah Sankey; Cindy Oswin

92 Angela Thorne *Susan Solstice*; Stephanie Beacham *Deborah Solstice*; Ian Ogilvy *Mark Solstice*; James Laurenson *Gregory Butler*

Happy Family Duke of York's 26 7 83

93 Derek Jacobi *Cyrano de Bergerac*; Floyd Bevan *Baron Christian de Neuvillette*

Cyrano de Bergerac Barbican 27 7 83

94 Pete Postlethwaite *Ragueneau*; Alice Krige *Roxane*; Derek Jacobi; John Bowe *Le Bret*

Cyrano de Bergerac Barbican 27 7 83

95 Antony Sher *Tartuffe*; Nigel Hawthorne *Orgon*

Tartuffe The Pit 28 7 83

96 Tricia Kelly; Amelda Brown; Linda Bassett; Cecily Hobbs

Fen Royal Court 29 7 83

97 Robin Lermitte *Alastair Yonge*; Anjela Belli *Davina Scott*

Bad Language Hampstead Theatre 18 83

98 Greg Hicks *Tony Kirby*; Gary Raymond *Paul Sycamore*; Ronald Hines *Mr Kirby*; Irene Sutcliffe *Mrs Kirby*; Jimmy Jewel *Martin Vanderhof*; Geraldine McEwan *Penelope Sycamore*

99 Rupert Frazer *Lt. Stefan Kovacs*; Michael Gough *Baron von Epp*; Alan Bates *Alfred Redl*

A Patriot for Me Theatre Royal, Haymarket 8 8 83

100 Giorgio Gennari *Polonius*; Gigi Dall'Aglio *Claudius*; Tiziana Rocchetta *Gertrude*; Gianpaolo Boccelli *Horatio*; Marcello Vazzoler *Yorick*

Hamlet Riverside 8 8 83

101 Peter McEnery *Antipholus of Ephesus*; Henry Goodman *Dromio of Ephesus*; John Dicks *Doctor Pinch*; Zoë Wanamaker *Adriana*

102 Jane Booker *Luciana*; Paul Greenwood *Antipholus of Syracuse*; Zoë Wanamaker

The Comedy of Errors Royal Shakespeare Theatre, Stratford 9 8 83

103 Richard O'Callaghan *Dromio of Syracuse*; Paul Greenwood; Paul Clayton *An Officer*   104 Zoë Wanamaker; Jane Booker

105 John Dicks *Solinus*; Timothy Kightley *Angelo*; Selena Carey-Jones *citizen*;
Joseph O'Conor *Aegeon*; Frankie Cosgrave *citizen*; Paul Clayton

The Comedy of Errors Royal Shakespeare Theatre, Stratford 9 8 83

106 Dickie Arnold *Old George*; Jenifer Landor *Emmie Hewins*; James Fleet *Joshua Farr*; Peggy Mount *Cal*; Ron Cook *Cookie Hewins*

107 Dickie Arnold; Campbell Morrison *Timmy Large*; Bruce Alexander *Black George*; Paul Basson *Young George Hewins*

The Dillen The Other Place 10 8 83

108 Dickie Arnold; Ron Cook; Carolyn Pickles *Emma Hewins*

109 *the pea pickers*

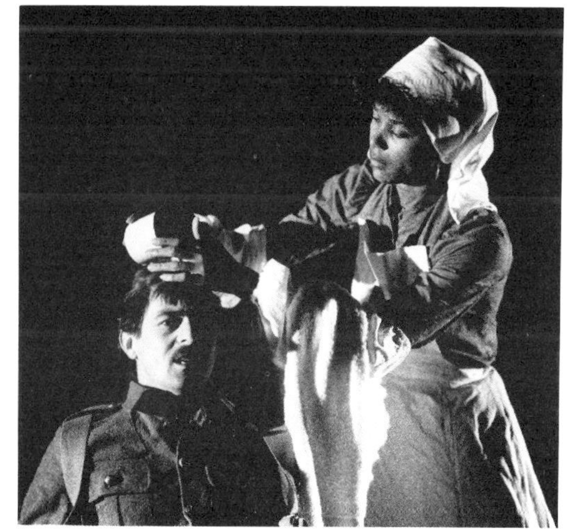

110 Ron Cook; Alphonsia Emmanuel *nurse*

The Dillen The Other Place 10 8 83

111 Ian McKellen *Boy*; Janet Suzman *Babe*

Cowardice Ambassadors 11 8 83

112 Hilary Reynolds *Agnes*; Susannah York *Doctor Martha Livingstone*; Honor Blackman *Mother Miriam Ruth*

Agnes of God Greenwich 17 8 83

113 Deborah Norton *Elspeth Grahame*

The Killing of Mr Toad Kings Head 23 8 83

114 Brian Deacon *Bernard*; Emma Piper *Josephine*; Glenda Jackson *Lotte*

Great and Small Vaudeville 25 8 83

115 Michael Gambon *Ödön von Horváth*; Ian McDiarmid *Bertolt Brecht*

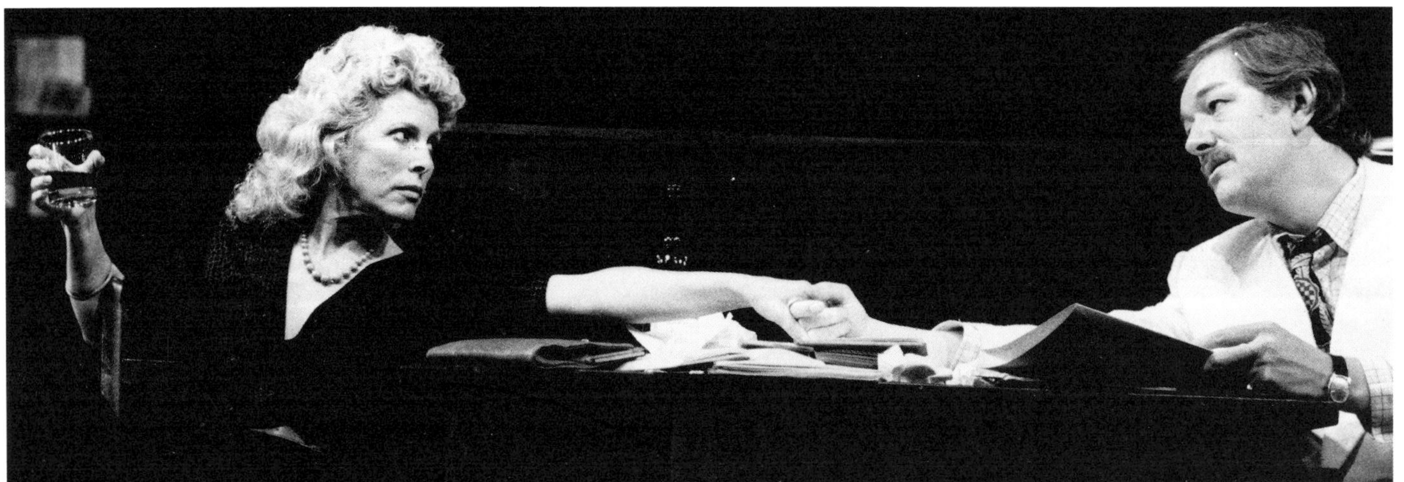

116 Billie Whitelaw *Nelly Mann*; Michael Gambon

Tales from Hollywood Olivier 1983

117 Jan Nowicki *Rogozhin*; Jerzy Radziwilowicz *Myshkin*

Nastasia Filipovna Riverside 6 9 83

118 centre: Christopher Guinee *Marmeladov*

119 Michael Pennington *Rodion Raskolnikov*

Crime and Punishment Lyric Hammersmith 7 9 83

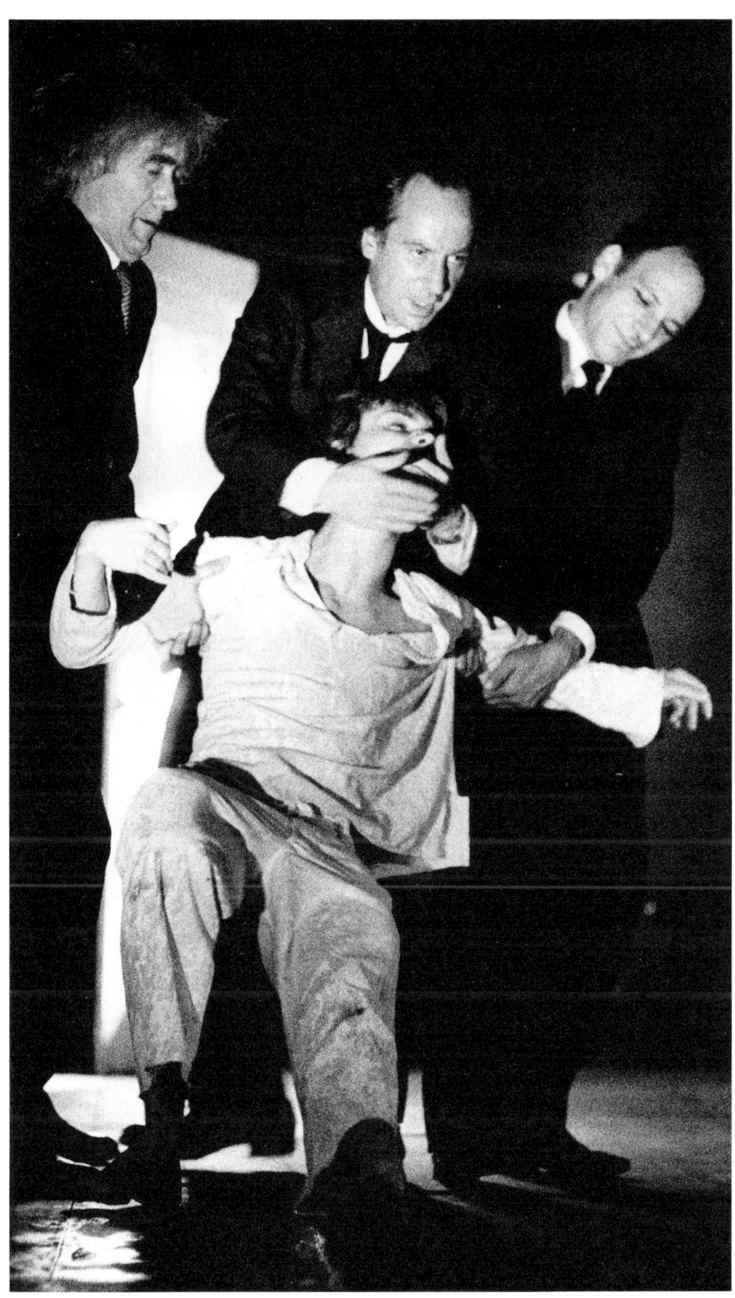

120 Ronald Forfar *Man with Axe*; Bill Paterson *Porfiry*; Joshua le Touzel *Mikolka*;
Peter Kelly *Zametov*

121 Paola Dionisotti *Katerina Ivanovna Marmeladov*;
Veronica Roberts *Sonia Marmeladov*

Crime and Punishment Lyric Hammersmith 7 9 83

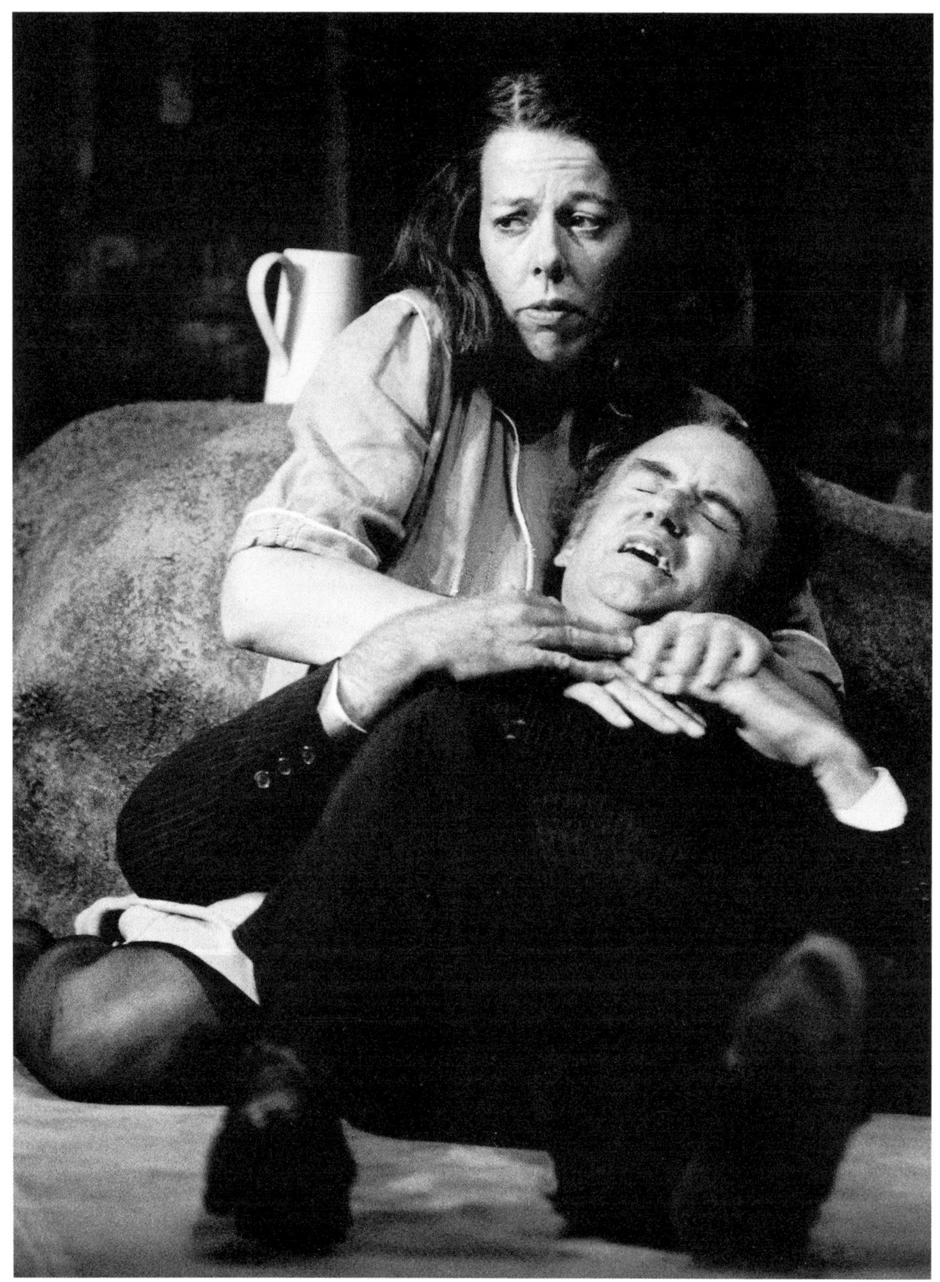

122 Frances de la Tour *Josie Hogan*; Ian Bannen *James Tyrone*

A Moon for the Misbegotten Mermaid 9 9 83

123 Trevor Eve *Leo Lehrer*; Joanne Whalley *Gilly Brown*

The Genius Royal Court 12 9 83

Production notes
Compiled by Michael Coveney

1 **Other Places** by Harold Pinter. Directed by Peter Hall, designed by John Bury. Judi Dench's award-winning performance in the third play of a triple bill, as a woman coming out of a coma after 29 years, set a high standard for the rest to aim at in the new theatre year.

2 **Rita, Sue and Bob Too** by Andrea Dunbar. Directed by Max Stafford-Clark, designed by Chris Townsend. Confirmation of Ms Dunbar's outstanding promise, as a frustrated husband gives free sex lessons to his adolescent babysitters. Part of the Young Writers' Festival.

3/4 **Major Barbara** by Bernard Shaw. Directed by Peter Gill, designed by Alison Chitty, music by Ilona Sekacz, lighting by Stephen Wentworth. Solid revival on a skeletal set, Brewster Mason's booming Undershaft for the NT less persuasive than his RSC version 12 years ago.

5 **Nuts** by Tom Topor. Presented by Graham Stewart, directed by David Gilmore, designed by Glenn Willoughby. Strong courtroom drama, Anne Twomey a welcome American visitor as an allegedly insane dame turned prostitute who has killed a client on the job. Nuffield Theatre, Southampton, transfer.

6 **Ducking Out** by Eduardo de Filippo in a version by Mike Stott. Directed by Mike Ockrent, designed by Poppy Mitchell, lighting by Leo Leibovici. Neapolitan Christmas fracas enjoyably transposed to Lancashire. Was this the first spaghetti northern? Transferred briefly to the Duke of York's (16 12 82).

7 **Ladies in Retirement** by Edward Percy and Reginald Denham. Presented by Paul Gane for Dela Avis Productions Ltd in association with Prince Loadsman. Tedious, doomed revival of 1939 thriller.

8 **A Handful of Dust** adapted from Evelyn Waugh's novel by Mike Alfreds. Presented by Shared Experience, directed by Mike Alfreds, designed by Paul Dart, music by Ilona Sekacz. A grey frieze of actors on a Georgian wall, ingeniously manipulated in Waugh's scenes of social whirl, country pleasures, domestic disintegration and nemesis in the Brazilian tropics.

9 **Diary of a Hunger Strike** by Peter Sheridan. Touring presentation of Hull Truck Theatre Company, directed by Pam Brighton, designed by Di Seymour. Harrowing, balanced account of the first martyr in the Northern Ireland hunger strikes of 1981.

10 **The Real Thing** by Tom Stoppard. Presented by Michael Codron, directed by Peter Wood, designed by Carl Toms, lighting by William Bundy, sound by Jonathan Deans.

11 **The Dead Class,** a dramatic seance devised and directed by Tadeusz Kantor. Images of inanimate youth and decrepit old age coalesce in a hypnotised, hypnotic classroom. Repeat London engagement for a Polish classic after six years.

12 **Man and Superman** by Bernard Shaw. Presented by Duncan C. Weldon with Paul Gregg and Lionel Becker for Triumph Apollo Productions in association with Keep Films Limited. Directed by Patrick Dromgoole, designed by Akache, costumes by Ann Curtis, lighting by Charlie Paton. Birmingham Repertory Theatre transfer.

13-15 **Paisley Patterns** by John Byrne. Presented by the Traverse Theatre, Edinburgh, directed by David Hayman, designed by John Byrne. The first of "The Slab Boys" trilogy dates from 1978, the last from 1982. Together they give a vivid, quirky picture of a Paisley community progressing from spotty adolescence in a 1957 carpet factory to grey disillusionment in the early '70s. Wonderful performances from Billy McColl and the Scottish company, many good jokes.

16 **Camelot** by Alan Jay Lerner (book and lyrics) and Frederick Loewe (music). The Mike Merrick and Don Gregory production presented by Paul Gregg and Lionel Becker for Apollo Theatre Productions. Directed by Michael Rudman, designed by Desmond Heeley, lighting by David Hersey. Excruciatingly tatty revival of 1960 musical partially redeemed by Richard Harris's effectively old-fashioned star performance.

17 **A Midsummer Night's Dream** by Shakespeare. Directed by Bill Bryden, designed by Bob Crowley, costumes by Deirdre Clancy, lighting by William Bundy, musical direction by John Tams. Victorian music-hall elements impinge on a dusty, nostalgic world of ancient faëry in a production that toured successfully before transferring, Robert Stephens replacing Scofield, to the Lyttelton (14 4 83).

18 **Steafel Variations** by Sheila Steafel and others. One-woman revue presented by Knightsbridge Productions Ltd that came a cropper after two weeks. Expressive zany in the wrong place.

19 **Messiah** by Martin Sherman. Directed by Ronald Eyre, designed by Yolande Sonnabend, lighting by Mick Hughes. A false Messiah in 17th-century Poland, a busy plot, a fine performance by Maureen Lipman. Transferred, disastrously, to the Aldwych (26 1 83).

20 **Clay** by Peter Whelan. Directed by Bill Alexander, designed by Poppy Mitchell, lighting by Michael Calf. Well-performed, old-fashioned play in a rural farmhouse hedged with intimations of the apocalypse.

21 **Twelfth Night** by Shakespeare. Presented by the London Shakespeare Group, directed by John Fraser, designed by Maxine Webster. Average production ideally suited to the extensive foreign touring demands made on it by the British Council.

22 **French Without Tears** by Terence Rattigan. Directed by Alan Strachan, designed by Peter Rice. Able revival of Rattigan's 1936 light comedy.

23 **Peter Pan** by J. M. Barrie. Directed by John Caird and Trevor Nunn, designed by John Napier, costumes by Andreane Neofitou, music by Stephen Oliver, lighting by David Hersey, fights by Malcolm Ranson.

24 **Nightingale** by Charles Strouse. Directed by Peter James, design and costumes (with Julia Fletcher) by Jenny Tiramani, musical direction by David Firman, choreography by Gillian Gregory. Charming opera derived from Hans Christian Andersen story, plangently Oriental, tastefully spectacular and well sung.

25/26 **Noises Off** by Michael Frayn. Presented by Michael Codron, directed by Michael Blakemore, designed by Michael Annals. Last year's outstanding comedy given a complete deluxe cast change and as triumphantly funny as ever.

27 **Mr Cinders** by Clifford Grey and Greatrex Newman, with additional lyrics by Leo Robin, music by Vivian Ellis and Richard Myers. Directed by Tony Craven, choreography by Kenn Oldfield, designed by Norman Coates, costumes by Marty Flood. Transferred to the Fortune (27 4 83).

28/29 **The School for Scandal** by Sheridan. Presented by Ducan C. Weldon with Paul Gregg and Lionel Becker for Triumph Apollo Productions by arrangement with Louis I. Michaels Ltd. Directed by John Barton with Peter Stevenson, designed by Christopher Morley, music by Guy Woolfenden, lighting by Brian Harris.

30 **Yakety Yak!** by Robert Walker based on the songs of Jerry Leiber and Mike Stoller. Presented by Christopher Malcolm in association with Carlin Music and Laurie Marsh on behalf of Another Artist Ltd. Directed by Robert Walker, designed by Andrew McAlpine and Gemma Jackson, lighting by Mark Pritchard, choreography by Lynne Hockney, musical direction by The Darts. Enjoyable anthology transferred from the Half Moon to cabaret conditions.

31 **Miss Julie** by Strindberg, translated by Michael Meyer. Directed by Clare Davidson, designed by Dermot Hayes, lighting by Dave Horn. Splendid revival with coruscating performances by Cheryl Campbell and Stephen Rea. Transferred to Duke of York's (2 3 83).

32 **The Messiah** by Patrick Barlow. Presented by the National Theatre of Brent. Directed by Jude Kelly, designed by Tom Cairns.

33 **The Vandalist** adapted by John Retallack and the company from Ubu Roi by Alfred Jarry, translated by Cyril Connolly. Presented by the Actors Touring Company, directed by John Retallack, designed by Wendy Freeman. First in a three month season of five plays.

34 **Any Minute Now . . .** by David MacLennan and David Anderson. Presented by the Wildcat Theatre Company, directed by Ian Wooldridge, designed by Alex Gorman, costumes by Nadia Arthur, lighting by Kris Misselbrook, additional songs by David Hicks.

35 **Quixote** by Cervantes, adapted by Richard Curtis and John Retallack. Presented by the Actors Touring Company, directed by John Retallack, designed by Poppy Mitchell and Janet Newton.

36 **A Map of the World** by David Hare. Directed by David Hare, designed by Hayden Griffin, lighting by Rory Dempster, music by Nick Bicât. Same production team as for the play's world premiere by the Sydney Theatre Company at the Adelaide Festival in March 1982.

37 **You Should See Us Now** by Peter Tinniswood. Directed by John Adams, designed by Bernard Culshaw, lighting by Leonard Tucker. Generally underestimated comedy of suburban couples regressing to childhood behaviour (and existence) in order to explain adult inadequacies. Often very funny, Giles Cooper-ish.

38 **Hard Feelings** by Doug Lucie. Presented by the Oxford Playhouse Company, directed by Mike Bradwell, designed by Geoff Rose, lighting by Raymond Cross.

39 **Charley's Aunt** by Brandon Thomas. Directed by Peter James and Peter Wilson, designed by Martin Sutherland, Douglas Bullock and Brenda Murphy, lighting by Dave Horn. 1895 farcical war horse well mounted by the genuinely funny Griff Rhys-Jones as the Oxford undergrad under drag. Transferred to the Aldwych (5 4 83).

40 **Secret Gardens** designed and directed by Tim Albery, Antony McDonald, Geraldine Pilgrim and Ian Spink. Music by Orlando Gough and Andrew Poppy, lighting by John Ricker. Inspired by an Edwardian children's novel by Frances Hodgson Burnett, the ICA's visual theatre policy was greeted with as much bafflement as delight.

41 **United States I-IV** performance by Laurie Anderson. Presented by the ICA, lighting by Jan Kroeze, projection by Perry Hoberman, sound by Bob Davies. Autobiographical eight-hour epic by the influential superstar who combines elements of late 70s theatrical avant garde with the music of new technology.

42 **Kick for Touch** by Peter Gill. Directed by Peter Gill, designed by Alison Chitty, lighting by Stephen Wentworth. Short, boring play notably well performed.

43 **Small Change** by Peter Gill. Directed by Peter Gill, decor by William Dudley, costumes by Alison Chitty, lighting by Stephen Wentworth. Good 1976 piece, a mosaic of friendship and tensions for sons and mothers. Three of the original cast joined by Maggie Steed.

44 **Lent** by Michael Wilcox. Directed by Christopher Fettes, designed by John Otto, lighting by Dave Horn. School memory play of allusive strangeness and insidious charm. Beautifully played and designed.

45 **Crystal Clear** devised by Phil Young and the cast. Presented by Robert Fox in association with Michael Medwin for Memorial Films. Directed by Phil Young, designed by David Burrows, lighting by Mick Hughes, costumes by Nadya Cohen. Old Red Lion, Islington, transfer.

46 **Heartbreak House** by Bernard Shaw. Presented by Duncan C. Weldon with Paul Gregg and Lionel Becker for Triumph Apollo Productions Ltd by arrangement with Louis I. Michaels Ltd. Directed by John Dexter, designed by Jocelyn Herbert, lighting by Andy Phillips.

47 **Call Me Madam** by Irving Berlin (music and lyrics), and Howard Lindsay and Russel Crouse (book). The Birmingham Rep production presented by Duncan C. Weldon with Paul Gregg and Lionel Becker for Triumph Apollo Productions Ltd by arrangement with Louis Benjamin for Stoll Moss Theatres Ltd, by arrangement with Chappell Music Ltd. Directed by Roger Redfarn, designed by Terry Parsons, choreography by Tudor Davies, musical direction by Ed Coleman, lighting by Graham Large.

48 **Lorenzaccio** by Alfred de Musset, translated and adapted by John Fowles. Directed by Michael Bogdanov, designed by John Gunter, costumes by Stephanie Howard, lighting by Chris Ellis, music by Stephen Oliver, fights by Malcolm Ranson.

49 **Mr Puntila and his servant Matti** by Brecht, translated by Paul Kriwaczek and Paul Lewis, adapted by Jeremy Brooks. Presented by Foco Novo, directed by Roland Rees, designed by Peter Hartwell, costumes by Sheelagh Killeen, lighting by Andy Phillips. Decent touring revival of one of Brecht's freshest and funniest plays.

50 **Marilyn!** by Jacques Wilson (book and lyrics) and Mort Garson (music). Presented by Gaylord, Elmo Williams and Elliott Kastner. Directed and choreographed by Larry Fuller, designed by David Hersey, costumes by Tazeena Firth, musical direction by Ray Cook.

51 **Short List** by Michael Rudman. Directed by Mike Ockrent, decor by Poppy Mitchell, costumes by Sheelagh Killeen, lighting by Mick Hughes. Slight first play by a director who sees the funny side of most things, including play competitions. In-jokes and bitchery galore.

52 **Victory** by Howard Barker. Presented by Joint Stock Theatre Group in association with the Royal Court. Directed by Danny Boyle, designed by Deirdre Clancy, lighting by Gareth Jones. Panoramic quasi-historical piece in the manner of Edward Bond. A Puritan widow (Julie Covington) seeks husband's corpse under and around the restored King Charles.

53 **Julius Caesar** by Shakespeare. Directed by Ron Daniels, designed by Farrah, costumes by Ann Curtis, music by Nigel Hess, lighting by Andre Tammes. The gimmick of a simultaneous video screening of the key public events was later dropped.

54 **The Time of Your Life** by William Saroyan. Directed by Howard Davies, designed by Bob Crowley, costumes by Allan Watkins, lighting by Leo Leibovici, musical direction by Keith Nichols. The main house opening to the Stratford season was totally eclipsed by the rapturous reception accorded the studio revival of a 1939 American dream play.

55 **Blood Brothers** by Willy Russell. Presented by Bob Swash by arrangement with the Liverpool Playhouse. Directed by Chris Bond and Danny Hillier, designed by Andy Greenfield, lighting by Jimmy Simmons, musical direction by Richard Spanswick, sound by Autograph. Liverpool Playhouse transfer.

56 **The Rivals** by Sheridan. Directed by Peter Wood, designed by John Gunter, costumes by Bruce Snyder, lighting by Robert Bryan, music by Dominic Muldowney. In the great breakfast scene, Michael Hordern's Sir Anthony Absolute is struck by remembrance of flings past. The line about lying like a cucumber on a hot bed was the most sublimely indecent of the year.

57 **Edmund Kean** by Raymund Fitzsimons. Directed by Alison Sutcliffe, designed by Martin Tilley, lighting by John Watt. Within a week of receiving his Oscar for Gandhi, Ben Kingsley, character actor par excellence, was back in London portraying one of the stage's great wild men. Kean himself would have still been at the party. Transferred to the Haymarket (13 6 83).

58 **Daisy Pulls It Off** by Denise Deegan. Presented by Andrew Lloyd Webber, directed by David Gilmore, designed by Glenn Willoughby, lighting by Brian Harris, school song by Beryl Waddle-Browne. Spirited pastiche of the Angela Brazil novels, jolly good gym-slipped fun with an anthem by an anagrammatical composer. Nuffield Theatre, Southampton, transfer.

59 **Twelfth Night** by Shakespeare. Directed by John Caird, designed by Robin Don, costumes by Alix Stone, lighting by David Hersey, music by Ilona Sekacz. No boxed foliage or cute topiary in this Illyria, but an old gnarled tree on a neo-classical clifftop.

60 **When the Wind Blows** by Raymond Briggs, adapted by him from his own book. Presented by Colin Brough for the Lupton Theatre Company Ltd by arrangement with Raymond Briggs and Snowman Enterprises Ltd. Directed by David Neilson, designed by Billy Meall, lighting by John A. Williams. Little Theatre, Bristol, transfer.

61 **The White Glove** by Richard Maher and Roger Michell. Directed by Roger Michell, designed by Chris Townsend. Holmes and Watson, posing as mining engineers, barge into the last scene of *The Cherry Orchard*. A promisingly original idea then went rapidly off the rails, and at great length.

62-66 **The Roaring Girl** by Thomas Middleton and Thomas Dekker. Directed by Barry Kyle, designed by Chris Dyer, music by Guy Woolfenden, lighting by Leo Leibovici, fights by Malcolm Ranson. 1608 Jacobean rarity spiritedly revived to corroborate T. S. Eliot's high opinion of it.

67 **The Body** by Nick Darke. Directed by Nick Hamm, designed by Dermot Hayes, music by Guy Woolfenden, lighting by Michael Calf. Rural and nuclear base communities in ominous clash over dead body shock horror.

68 **The Trojan War Will Not Take Place** by Jean Giraudoux translated by Christopher Fry. Directed by Harold Pinter, designed by Eileen Diss, costumes by Robin Fraser Paye, lighting by Mick Hughes, music by Harrison Birtwistle. Ghastly, boring evening unredeemed even by the ambiguously enchanting Helen of Nicola Pagett.

69 **Other Worlds** by Robert Holman. Directed by Richard Wilson, designed by John Byrne, lighting by Matthew Richardson. Yorkshire during the Napoleonic wars, fishermen at odds with farmers, and an imprisoned ape hanged as a Frenchman.

70 **Merrily We Roll Along** by Stephen Sondheim (music and lyrics) and George Furth (book), based on the original play by George S. Kaufman and Moss Hart. Presented by the Guildhall School of Music and Drama by arrangement with Joseph Weinberger Ltd on behalf of Music Theatre International of New York. Directed by Ian Judge, designed by Akache, musical staging by Sheila Falconer, musical direction by Firoz Shapur, lighting by George Owczarski, costumes by Daphne Newington. New York flop (16 performances at the end of 1981) gloriously restored by student production first seen at the Guildhall School of Music and Drama (28 3 83).

71 **Crimes of the Heart** by Beth Henley. Directed by Simon Stokes, designed by Poppy Mitchell, lighting by Bart Cossee. Pulitzer Prize winning play first seen at the Louisville, Kentucky new plays festival in 1979 before moving to Broadway.

72 **Beethoven's Tenth** by Peter Ustinov. Presented by Duncan C. Weldon with Paul Gregg and Lionel Becker for Triumph Apollo Productions Ltd in association with Alexander H. Cohen. Directed by Robert Chetwyn, designed by Kenneth Mellor, costumes by John Fraser, lighting by Graham Large, music by Stephen Pruslin. Birmingham Rep transfer, following tour.

73 **Bugsy Malone** adapted from Alan Parker's film by Michael Dolenz, music and lyrics by Paul Williams. Presented by Martin Gates and Philip Summerscales for Harcourt Theatrical Productions in association with A & M Records, by arrangement with Louis Benjamin for Stoll Moss Theatres Ltd. Directed by Michael Dolenz, designed by Ralph Koltai, choreography by Gillian Gregory, lighting by Joe Davis, musical direction by Barry Westcott, costumes by Annena Stubbs. Kids' stuff.

74 **The Dining Room** by A. R. Gurney Jr. Directed by Alan Strachan, designed by Bernard Culshaw, lighting by Mick Hughes. One of the year's best, most distinctive plays. Why no transfer?

75 **Men Should Weep** by Ena Lamont Stewart. Presented by the 7:84 Theatre Company (Scotland), directed by Giles Havergal, designed by Geoff Rose, costumes by Morna Baxter, lighting by Gerry Jenkinson. One of the hits of the 1982 Edinburgh Festival, giving stylish flair to a slice of Glasgow tenements life in the 1930s. This 'lost' 1947 piece prompted comparisons with Odets and O'Casey.

76 **Falkland Sound/Voces de Malvinas** based on the letters of David Tinker and interviews conducted by the company, edited by Louise Page. Directed by Max Stafford-Clark, designed by David Roger, lighting by Simon Byford.

77-79 **Henry VIII** by Shakespeare. Directed by Howard Davies, designed by Hayden Griffin, costumes by Deirdre Clancy, lighting by David Hersey, music by Ilona Sekacz, choreography by Stuart Hopps.

80 **Woza Albert!** conceived by Percy Mtwa, Mbongeni Ngema and Barney Simon. Presented by Terence Frisby and the Market Theatre, Johannesburg, by arrangement with Ian B. Albery. Directed and designed by Barney Simon.

81 **Inner Voices** by Eduardo de Filippo, translated by N F Simpson. Directed by Mike Ockrent, designed by Raimonda Gaetani, lighting by Leonard Tucker. Sir Ralph's semi-somnolent briskness well used in an otherwise damp squib set in post-War Naples.

82 **Exit the King** by Eugene Ionesco, translated by Donald Watson. Directed by Christopher Fettes, designed by John Otto, lighting by Dave Horn. 1962 revival which failed to make new friends.

83/84 **A New Way to Pay Old Debts** by Philip Massinger. Directed by Adrian Noble, designed by Bob Crowley, music by Colin Sell, lighting by Leo Leibovici. The Other Place maintained standards with this rapturously received Jacobean revival.

85 **Buried Inside Extra** by Thomas Babe. Directed by Joseph Papp, designed by Mike Boak, lighting by Ralph K. Holmes, costumes by Theoni V. Aldredge. Exchange visit of the New York Shakespeare Festival production at the Public after we sent them Top Girls.

86 **Y** musical spectacular conceived by Jean Marie Riviere, Arturo Brachetti, Pierre Simonini and Caroline Roboh. Presented by Vladimir Forgency by arrangement with Ian B. Albery. Directed by Jean Marie Riviere, designed by Pierre Simonini, choreography by Molly Molloy, music by Frederic Botton, lighting by Claude Tissier, costumes by Roberto Rosello.

87 **Mizu No Eki** by Shogo Ohta. Presented by the Tenkei Theatre Company, directed by Shogo Ohta, lighting by Haruhiko Tsujimoto. Updated Noh in slow motion silent traffic round a watering hole.

88 **The Winslow Boy** by Terence Rattigan. Directed by Michael Rudman, designed by Carl Toms, lighting by Dave Horn. Competent, over-praised production of schematic flatly written 1946 war horse.

89 **Little Lies** by Joseph George Caruso, freely adapted from Pinero's *The Magistrate*. Presented by Robert Mackintosh for Full Steam Ahead Productions Ltd by arrangement with Ian B. Albery and by special arrangement with William de Silva and Betsy Rosenfield and Joel Spector for Productions International Corporation. Directed by Tony Tanner, designed by Joe Vanek, lighting by Mick Hughes. Excruciatingly unfunny performance by John Mills in an unnecessary adaptation of Pinero's farce. No style. Watford Palace transfer.

90 **The Fawn** by John Marston. Directed by Giles Block, designed by Poppy Mitchell, lighting by Rory Dempster, music by David Bedford. Pointless revival of 1604 curiosity that failed to arouse mine.

91 **Rococo** by Peter Godfrey. Devised and presented by Rational Theatre. Directed by Andy Wilson and Jim Whiting, designed by Sandy Powell. Gorgeously decadent visual extravaganza poking its tongue out at Restoration comedy mannerisms in high wire coiffures. Made a change.

92 **Happy Family** by Giles Cooper. Presented by Dramatis Personae Ltd in association with the Windsor Theatre Company. Directed by Maria Aitken, designed by Hayden Griffin, costumes by Caroline Amies, lighting by Rory Dempster. Decent revival of quirky 1966 comedy by the late playwright primarily known for his radio work and his bizarre exodus from an express train.

93/94 **Cyrano de Bergerac** by Edmond Rostand, translated by Anthony Burgess. Directed by Terry Hands, designed by Ralph Koltai, costumes by Alexander Reid, music by Nigel Hess, lighting by Terry Hands and Clive Morris, fights by Ian McKay, nose by Christopher Tucker. Extravagant, spectacular, romantic and swashbuckling. Tripartite triumph for director, company and Jacobi.

95 **Tartuffe** by Moliere, translated by Christopher Hampton. Directed by Bill Alexander, designed by Alison Chitty, lighting by Leo Leibovici. Rippling new translation with a fine duel between the daemonic Sher and the resilient, prickly Hawthorne.

96 **Fen** by Caryl Churchill. Presented by Joint Stock Theatre Company, directed by Les Waters, designed by Annie Smart, lighting by Tom Donnellan. First seen at the Almeida (16 2 83), the play returned to London after an extensive tour and successful visit to the Public Theatre, New York. Ghosts and passion on the appropriated fenland of East Anglia provided a strangely hypnotic play, cannily designed and directed. Good versatile cast.

97 **Bad Language** by Dusty Hughes. Directed by Mike Bradwell, designed by Geoff Rose. Parochial pleasures of cossetted Cambridge students.

98 **You Can't Take It With You** by Moss Hart and George S. Kaufman. Directed by Michael Bogdanov, designed by Grant Hicks, costumes by Ruth Myers, lighting by Howard Eaton. 1936 comedy patchily revived in the wake of a Broadway version earlier in 1983.

99 **A Patriot for Me** by John Osbone. Presented by Duncan C. Weldon with Paul Gregg and Lionel Becker for Triumph Apollo Productions Ltd in association with Proscenium Productions Ltd and Center Theatre Group – Ahmanson Los Angeles, by arrangement with Louis I. Michaels Ltd. Directed by Ronald Eyre, designed by Carl Toms, lighting by Mark Henderson, music by Ilona Sekacz. Notably triumphant revival of 1965 cause célèbre at the Royal Court which opened this year's Chichester Festival Theatre season (11 5 83).

100 **Hamlet** by Shakespeare. Presented by the Compagnia del Colletivo di Parma, Italy, visiting the second London International Festival of Theatre. Free, exuberant, funny adaptation performed in Italian, part of a trilogy that has been three years in the preparation.

101 -105 **The Comedy of Errors** by Shakespeare. Directed by Adrian Noble, designed by Ultz, lighting by Robert Bryan, music by Nigel Hess. Following the traditional RSC justifiably irreverent attitude towards this comedy, Noble's production, as were those of Clifford Williams and Trevor Nunn, is a riot of fresh and rollicking invention from the word go.

106-110 **The Dillen** adapted by Ron Hutchinson from the book by Angela Hewins. Directed by Barry Kyle, design and costumes (with Jackie Gunn) by Chris Dyer, music researched and composed by Guy Woolfenden, lighting by Leo Leibovici. Ambitious, peripatetic production that spilled through the town tracing the life of a local man, George Hewins, down the century and through the wars. Local residents and artisans joined in, making the resonant point that not only Shakespeare lived by the Avon.

111 **Cowardice** by Sean Mathias. Presented by Duncan C. Weldon with Paul Gregg and Lionel Becker for Triumph Apollo Productions Ltd in association with Ian McKellen Productions Ltd. Directed by Anthony Page, designed by Hayden Griffin, costumes by Deirdre Clancy, music by Martin Duncan, lighting by Rory Dempster. Real stinker of a new play about a brother and sister who pretend they're Noel and Gertie. Suburban melodramatic camp.

112 **Agnes of God** by John Pielmeier. Presented by Bill Kenwright and Alan Cluer by arrangement with Kenneth Waissman and Lou Kramer. Directed by Frank Hauser, designed by Claire Lyth, lighting by Dave Horn. Unadulterated tosh with religioso pretensions about novitiate who has allegedly strangled the result of an immaculate conception. Mother Superior and court-appointed psychiatrist fiddle about in attendance. Not the best advertisement we have received for the new plays festival in Louisville, Kentucky.

113 **The Killing of Mr Toad** by David Gooderson. Directed by Peter Watson, designed by Laurie Dennett, costumes by Maggie Smith, musical direction by Robb Stewart. Quirky, promising first play about the dark side of the life of Kenneth Grahame, author of *The Wind in the Willows*, as viewed by his wife, Rat, Mole, Badger and Toad. Salisbury Playhouse transfer.

114 **Great and Small** by Botho Strauss, translated by David Essinger. Presented by Duncan C. Weldon with Paul Gregg and Lionel Becker for Triumph Apollo Productions Ltd, directed by Keith Hack, designed by Voytek, lighting by Graham Large, music by Ben Mason. British premiere of 1979 piece by Peter Stein's dramaturg at the Berlin Schaubuhne.

115/116 **Tales from Hollywood** by Christopher Hampton. Directed by Peter Gill, designed by Alison Chitty, lighting by Stephen Wentworth, music by Terry Davies. First seen at the Mark Taper Forum, Los Angeles, in March 1982.

117 **Nastasia Filipovna** adapted from the last chapters of Dostoyevsky's *The Idiot*, and directed, by Andrzej Wajda. This production by the Stary Theatre of Cracow came hotfoot to London from the Edinburgh Festival. The work of two leading Eastern European directors, each tackling the same great Russian novelist, was thus, by an extraordinary coincidence, unveiled in the capital on successive nights.

118/121 **Crime and Punishment** by Dostoyevsky, adapted by Yuri Lyubimov and Yuri Kariakin. English version by Nicholas Rzhevsky. Directed by Yuri Lyubimov, designed by David Borovsky. Guest production by the founding director of Moscow's distinguished Na Taganke Theatre.

122 **A Moon For the Misbegotten** by Eugene O'Neill. A Riverside Studios production, directed by David Leveaux, designed by Brien Vahey, lighting by Rory Dempster. First seen at the Riverside Studios (21 6 83), this memorable revival of O'Neill's 1943 swansong was booked for a ten-week season. David Leveaux then travelled, at the invitation of Robert Brustein's American Repertory Theatre, to direct the same piece with a different cast in the Loeb Theatre, Boston.

123 **The Genius** by Howard Brenton. Directed by Danny Boyle, designed by Peter Hartwell, lighting by Gareth Jones, sound by Patrick Bridgeman. Our theatre year ends with a truly outstanding new play about a contemporary, cocaine-sniffing Galileo in the damp Midlands on secondment from America. The place of pure research in the nuclear age is given bold theatrical metaphor in a breathtaking production, Trevor Eve consolidating his reputation as one of our very best young actors. Einstein's fears about the consequences of horrifying scientific discovery were never more pertinent than today. And Brenton's rich fabric is also shot through with sustained, exciting debate about the function of education in our universities and the morality of those who dispense it. A wonderful evening in the theatre: bright, tough, urgent and often very funny.

Alphabetical list of performers

Alphabetical list of productions